Cognitive Behavioral Therapy

Learn How to Use CBT and the Power of the Mind to Overcome Negative Thinking, Addiction, Depression, Phobias, Anxiety and Panic Disorders

By D.C. Johnson

I0438653

Table of Contents

Introduction

The mind is a terrible thing to waste, and unfortunately that's what the majority of people are doing day by day as they live lives in prisons of anxiety, depression, addiction and mental illness. I want to encourage you as you read this that there is a way out, life doesn't have to be like this forever. First, I want to congratulate you for taking the first steps on your road to recovery. The simple fact that you are prepared to take the time out and read this book is evidence enough that you are ready for a change. Therefore, I have every confidence that you are going to have the power to eradicate the demons out of out of your life.

The first step to being cured is admitting that you have a problem; I believe you've got over that hurdle or you wouldn't be reading this book. You may have already been diagnosed but are unable to afford the treatment which has led you to seek out self help books. You may not have been diagnosed but you know enough to determine that you have a problem. Whatever your reason, you have come to the right place and you are going to be able to get the help that you need.

Cognitive behavioral therapy (CBT) is one of the most effective treatments for all types of mental and emotional disorders. The bottom line is that every problem that you are ever going to have originates in the mind. Addiction is a state of mind, anxiety is a state of mind, depression is a state of mind. If you can control the way you think, you can overcome any of these conditions. May I warn you, CBT isn't for the faint hearted, and if you are looking for your typical therapy session then this definitely isn't it. You have to be strong willed and strong minded to embark on this journey because it's life long, there are no magic pills with CBT.

I want you to get better, my heart breaks when I see people suffering when they don't have to.

However, I trust that by the time you get to the end of this book you'll have the strength of a lion and you will be able to take on the world.

Chapter 1: What is Cognitive Behavioral Therapy?

Cognitive behavioral therapy (CBT) is a goal-orientated, short-term psychotherapy treatment that takes a practical hands on approach to problem solving. Its main aim is to change the thinking and behavior patterns that are behind the issues that people are facing, which will then lead to changing the way the individual feels. It is used to treat several psychological illnesses including depression, anxiety, drug or alcohol abuse and sleeping difficulties. CBT works by altering a person's behavior and attitudes by focusing on beliefs, thoughts and images that are held. This is referred to as 'cognitive processes,' and they are analyzed to discover how a person deals with emotional problems.

One of the major advantages of CBT is that therapy only lasts between five to ten months after which time patients have overcome their psychological issues. Patients typically attend one 50 minute session per week during which time the individual works with a therapist to determine the extent of the issue and what strategies will be the most effective for their unique condition. CBT equips patients with a set of principles that they will be able to use for a lifetime to deal with any psychological problems they may face.

Cognitive behavioral therapy is a combination of behavioral and psychotherapy. Psychotherapy focuses on how thinking patterns are established during childhood. The main aim of behavioral therapy is to evaluate the relationship between our thoughts, behavior and our problems. The majority of psychotherapists who specialize in CBT will customize the required therapy to the specific needs of the each patient. In other words, there is no one shoe fits all approach because every individual is different.

The Origin of Cognitive Behavioral Therapy

During the 1960's, psychiatrist Aaron Beck was the first person to recognize that there is a link between our thoughts and feelings. He began to notice that during his sessions, his patients had an internal dialogue but they would not disclose all of what they were thinking to him. For example, during a therapy session, a patient might be thinking: "The therapist isn't speaking much today, I wonder if he's angry with me?" These thoughts then make the client feel angry or anxious and respond to their thoughts with another thought that might go something like: "Maybe he's tired, or maybe it's because what I'm talking about isn't important." The second thought might help to change how he felt after the first thought.

Beck coined the term "automatic thoughts" to describe emotionally charged thoughts that can take over the mind. Beck discovered that people are not always aware of these thoughts, but they could learn how to identify them and then talk about them. If an individual was feeling upset for any reason, the thoughts were typically negative. Beck found that when a patient was able to identify these thoughts they were able to overcome the issues that they were dealing with.

Beck later termed it cognitive therapy because of the emphasis that it places on thinking. Today it is referred to as cognitive behavioral therapy because it has been combined with behavioral techniques. CBT has been assessed though numerous scientific trials to determine its validity and it has been found to be a very successful strategy for overcoming psychological issues.

The Treatment Process

Cognitive behavioral therapy is unique in that there is a set structure to each session as opposed to a patients just talking about whatever they feel like talking about. At the beginning of a session, the individual meets with the therapist to discuss the problems that the patient is facing and the goals that they want to work towards. These issues and goals act as the foundation for the sessions. Both client and therapist will discuss what they want to work on for the week; they will also discuss any conclusions from the session before. They will evaluate the progress that has been made with the assignment that was set from the previous session and then plan more assignments for further progress.

Assignments

Homework assignments are a critical component of cognitive behavioral therapy and what it involves will vary. For example, when the therapy first begins the patient might be asked to keep a journal of any feelings and incidents that lead to depression and anxiety so that they can analyze the thoughts that surround that incident. As the therapy progresses, another assignment may include exercises to handle specific incidents.

Why Structure is Important

Structure within a session is essential, it helps to ensure that time is utilized effectively. It also ensures that crucial information is not overlooked and that the client and the therapist can discuss new assignments that are related to the session.

To begin with, the therapist plays an active role in structuring the session. As the patient progresses and starts to gain more of an understanding of the principles that are most effective, they begin to take on more responsibility in terms of how the sessions are structured. The main aim of this method is so that at the end of the sessions the patient feels confident enough to keep working independently.

Group Sessions

Cognitive behavioral therapy is typically one to one; however, it also works well as a group therapy where families or groups with similar problems can get together and share their difficulties. This often seems daunting at first for many patients but once the sessions gets going individuals often draw great benefits from it. The group also provides valuable support and advice to one another because they can better understand what they are experiencing collectively.

How CBT is Different From Other Therapies

Cognitive behavioral therapy is specifically different to other therapies because of the nature of the client and therapist relationship. The majority of therapists encourage their patients to be dependent upon them. The patient then begins to see the therapist as the only person who has the answer to their problems when the reality is that the answer lies within them. The relationship that is developed within CBT is almost business like, both parties are bringing something to the table. The therapy will often ask the client for feedback so that they can improve their skills, they want to know whether the principles they are teaching their patients are actually helping them.

Beck came up with the term 'Collaborative empiricism,' this concept is focused on the patient and the therapist working together to discover how CBT is actually enhancing the life of the patient as opposed to them being in therapy for a lifetime, together they work out the best strategies to overcome their problems even when they outside of the office.

What Type of People Benefit From Cognitive Behavioral Therapy?

Anyone who has some type of psychological issue and is determined to get better. It doesn't work for everyone because there are some people who are content in staying in their mess. They would rather take medication or rely on their weekly visits to their psychiatrist. However, it takes a certain type of character to go through CBT. Patients are informed during their initial consultation what is required of them to overcome their particular issue. The therapist is generally capable of discerning whether or not an individual is a candidate for CBT or not and they will tell you from the onset whether it will work for you and advise other treatment options for those less suitable. If you are suffering from any of the following issues CBT will help you to overcome your problems:

- Sleep disorders
- Sex addiction
- Relationship issues
- Post traumatic stress disorder
- Phobias
- Obsessive compulsive disorder
- Mood swings
- Bad habits
- Health problems
- Eating disorders
- Depression
- Chronic pain
- Anxiety
- Negative thinking
- Chronic fatigue syndrome
- Childhood problems

- Adolescent problems
- Anger management

At present there is a growing interest in combining cognitive behavioral therapy with medication to assist people who suffer from delusions, hallucinations and other more serious psychological issues. Your therapist will be able to determine whether you are a candidate for this combination or not. It is not as easy to solve long term issues that have been embedded into the subconscious of the individual through short term therapy. However, patients can implement a range of principles that will assist them in improving their quality of life. Self help literature is also very inspirational and patients are advised to read recommended books that will further assist them in overcoming their problems.

Why do I Need to do Assignments

The people who are willing to put in the extra work outside of their time with a therapist are those who are most likely to benefit from CBT.

We will go more in-depth with this in a later chapter but people who suffer from depression will often state that they do not want to participate on work or social activities until they feel better. CBT will introduce them to a different way of thinking and encourage them to get involved in small activities that are not so overwhelming. They often find that it is partaking in social events that makes them feel better as opposed to waiting until they feel better before getting involved.

If an individual is willing to try the suggestion, their assignment will involve something like meeting up with a friend for lunch. An individual who takes this first step will make faster progress than someone who prefers to sit and talk about their problems instead of taking action.

Cognitive Behavioral Therapy and Its Effectiveness

It has been scientifically proven that CBT has the ability to alleviate the symptoms of the majority of emotional disorders. It is just as good, or possibly better than putting a patient on medication. One of the main reasons for this is that medication can become addictive, and because a patient hasn't learned to master their condition but they have become dependent on the chemicals induced by the medication once they stop taking it, they are right back to square one.

When CBT patients are monitored after a few years of having therapy it is often found that there have been substantial benefits. For example, only 12 sessions of cognitive behavioral therapy can help a patient to overcome depression just as well as medication throughout the follow-up period. The research demonstrates that CBT helps to bring about a real transformation in the mind of a patient and that continuous therapy or medication is not necessary. It is this that has fueled such a major interest in cognitive behavioral therapy.

There have also been comparisons with other short term psychological therapies such as social skills training and inter-personal therapy. All of which have proven to be equally as effective, there is now a drive to make more therapies as effective as CBT.

Cognitive behavioral therapy isn't some type of magical cure, not everyone can administer this type of therapy and practitioners must be exceptionally well trained. The client must be prepared to put in the work if they want to overcome. Getting over severe emotional trauma isn't something that's going to happen overnight.

Sometimes a 12 week time frame isn't going to be long enough. If a patient has been suffering from emotional disturbances for a considerable length of time it may take a lot longer to get to the root of the problem and then start working on the solution. However, one fact remains, and this is that CBT is rapidly developing within the field of psychology. New ideas are being researched to handle more difficult and deep rooted psychological issues.

Cognitive Behavioral Therapy and How it Works

Cognitive behavioral therapy is extremely complex and there is no easy answer to the question. There are a number of different theories as to how it works and there is a possibility that a number of strategies work together simultaneously to help an individual overcome their unique set of problems. Here are some of the methods used during cognitive behavioral therapy.

Learning Different Coping Methods

The main aim of CBT is to teach people the skills they need to overcome their problems without having to rely on weekly therapy visits. For example, a person who suffers from anxiety (an area that will be discussed in depth later on) will learn how to avoid certain situations to alleviate their fears. Confronting their fears in a manageable and gradual way will give the patient the confidence they need that will give them the ability to cope with their problem.

A person who is depressed may learn to monitor their thoughts through journaling and look at them from a more realistic standpoint. This helps them to understand why their mood is constantly in a downward spiral of decline. A person who finds it difficult to relate to others may learn to evaluate the assumptions they make about other people as opposed to always assuming the worst about a person.

Changing Beliefs and Behaviors

The client suffering from anxiety may move onto learn how to avoid what makes them anxious. During this process it will lead them to realize that their anxiety is not as threatening as they assumed. Someone who is depressed may eventually learn to see themselves as a regular member of society who has the potential to achieve great things in life as opposed to someone who is inferior and incapable of becoming a productive member of society. On a more basic level, they may come to understand that their thoughts are nothing more than thoughts and that they have the power to change them.

A New Type of Patient Therapist Relationship

One to one cognitive behavioral therapy introduces the client to a relationship they may not have had access to in other types of therapy. 'The collaborative style' gives them an active role in their transformation. The therapist is interested in their point of view and their reactions which then gives the therapy a definite focus and structure. The individual may feel that they are able to reveal their personal issues because they don't feel as if they are being judged as some lowly being who has a mountain of problems. This then enables them to arrive at the most appropriate decisions. Every individual is free to decide what is best for them because deep down they know. They want to get better, the answers are generally within them and they don't need anyone to tell them. Once a patient realizes this they feel empowered that they can implement the principles learned outside of the therapy room.

Problem Solving Skills

The methods implemented by cognitive therapy enable patients to solve long standing problems that they didn't believe could ever improve. For example, a person suffering from anxiety may work in a job that is boring and repetitive and not have the confidence to look for a position that is more suited to their actual skill set. A person suffering from depression may feel that they will never be good enough to make friends or to meet new people because no one is going to like them. An individual who is stuck in a relationship that they are not satisfied with may find a new way of resolving their disputes. Cognitive behavioral therapy will teach people how to deal with the root cause of their issues which in turn makes problem solving for their current issues much easier.

Do I Have to See a Therapist?

This all depends on the individual and that is the reason why I have written this book because I do believe that not everyone has to see a therapist to benefit from cognitive behavioral therapy. There are a lot of self help books written by trained professionals who have broken the most effective techniques down into layman's terms. Such books are for people who know what their problem is and are ready to go ahead and do what is necessary to overcome their issues. However, there are some people who need a bit more guidance. I believe if you are reading this book you are one of those individuals who is ready to start your journey towards healing without the help of a therapist. If this sounds like you, keep reading.

Chapter 2: The Power of the Mind

The Basics of Mind Power

I was abused as a child, I was raped as a teenager, my parents were alcoholics....... I could continue but I think you understand the point that I am trying to make. These are the excuses that people make for their failure in life. They are legitimate reasons to suffer from depression or anxiety; however, if you want to improve your life you are going to have to understand that these things are in the past. Even if the event happened yesterday, it's in the past and dwelling on it is only going to become a hindrance to you in life. If you were to take a pen and paper and list reasons why you are in the situation that you are in right now everything would point to some external factor outside of yourself. So now that you have come to the realization that you have spent the last 20 years playing the blame game, now it's time to look within. In this chapter I am going to reveal to you the power that your mind has to create your reality, in other words you thought yourself into addiction, you thought yourself into depression, you thought yourself into anxiety. Whatever negative state of mind you are in, nobody put you in it but yourself.

Our entire physical reality is constructed out of energy and this includes our thoughts, this is not a theory, this is not a concept, it is a reality revealed to us through quantum physics. The way you think has a powerful effect on everything that happens in your life.

The majority of us go through life paying little to no attention to the way we think, how the mind works, why we are fearful of certain things, what we pay attention to and what we ignore. We tend to go with the flow and accept things the way they are. We travel through life neglecting one of the most powerful tools that we have, and that is our mind.

You Attract What You Focus On

You have the power to direct your mind towards a specific outcome. Whether it is the outcome that you want or the outcome that you don't want, your mind will attract it depending on what it is focused on. If you focus on depressing thoughts you will attract depressing situations into your life. Mind power is having a firm understanding of these principles and making our thoughts work in our favor. Your thoughts are the main creative forces in your life, when you make a conscious decision to think well about your situation you will awaken an entire new life of opportunity and power.

Your New Life is Dependent Upon Your Mind

If you want to make changes in your life, you are going to have to change the way you use your mind. You can't think negative and positive thoughts simultaneously because one of those thought patterns is going to dominate. Human beings are creatures of habit and our minds are always going to revert back to what we know.

Therefore, we must make a conscious effort to ensure that our positive thoughts and emotions are the dominating force in our lives.

It Starts From The Inside Out

No amount of plastic surgery and working out at the gym is going to make you feel better about yourself. You can have the most beautiful woman in the world, or the most handsome man in the world with the most despicable insides. Their thought processes are so jacked up that even though it appears they have got everything together because of the way they look they are still depressed. Have you ever wondered why rich people commit suicide? They have achieved what the majority of the world never will, society teaches us that material possessions and status will make us happy but that's clearly a lie or some of the most seemingly successful people in the world wouldn't be so miserable that they resort to suicide. You will often hear the same story, and that is they were battling with depression and addiction for many years. In other words they hadn't managed to drown out that inner negative force and it was the dominant force in their life. Their thought process meant that they had no peace. Therefore, we can conclude that changing external circumstances is pointless unless it is accompanied by a transformation in our thoughts and our belief system.

In order to overcome any type of psychological or emotional condition, you are going to have to train your conscious mind to think thoughts of peace, happiness and joy. Learn to eliminate negativity such as worry and fear by keeping your conscious mind busy with expecting the best out of life and make sure that the thoughts that dominate your mind are the ones that you want to see come to pass in your life.

The Subconscious Mind

Everybody knows that we have a subconscious mind, but for the majority of us the knowledge stops there. Your subconscious mind is the one that you are not consciously aware of, it is the one that is hidden, but exists inside of you. It picks up the dominant thoughts that come from your conscious mind and its job is to attract the circumstances that mirror the images that you are projecting from within.

You Reap What You Sow

Think of your subconscious mind as soil that is extremely fertile and any seed that you plant in it will take route and start to grow. The thoughts that you think about continuously are the seeds that you are sowing. Just as apple trees produce apples and oranges produce oranges your mind will produce exactly what it thinks about. Whatever you put in, is what you get out, reaping and sowing is a law.

Your conscious mind is the keeper that looks after the soil and you are responsible for being knowledgeable of how this process works. You do this by wisely choosing the thoughts that you allow to seep into your subconscious mind. For the majority of us, our position as a keeper has never been explained. Due to our ignorance, we have allowed weeds to grow that have chocked the life out of any of the good seeds that may have been planted.

The subconscious mind doesn't take inventory of what it allows in because it doesn't have the power to do so; it opens the door to anything that is presented to it. In other words, it will attract misfortune, ill health, and failure just as easily as it will attract health, abundance and success. Your subconscious welcomes everything that is presented to it with repetition and feeling regardless of whether these thoughts are negative or positive. It is not capable of evaluating things in the same way that your conscious mind is able to. This is why it is imperative that you are attentive to what you are thinking about.

Synchronicity

Once you have grasped hold of the fact that your subconscious mind will latch onto to anything that you desire or need and you begin to work towards projecting the images that you want and need. You will notice that random positive incidents will start to take place in your life. To the mind that has not been trained, random events are down to luck or coincidence but there is no such thing as either of them. It is simply the manifestation of the energy that you have set into motion as a result of your thoughts. This powerful assistant working alongside your conscious mind will lead you to the circumstances and the people required to cause everything that you desire to come to pass.

We All Have a Part to Play

Modern physics views the universe as a massive conjoined web of electric activity. The universe is not only a living and breathing organism that is changing constantly, but everything that is in the universe has an effect on everything else. At the most basic level, the universe appears to be a just one big ocean of energy that just exists. However, scientists are now authenticating what so called seers and mystics have been trying to tell us for thousands of years, human beings are not alienated from the universe; we are all a part of one greater whole.

We know that the universe and everything in it is made up of energy. Everything from your thoughts to the items that you keep in your home are made up of energy. This means that whatever created the universe also created your mind with the exact same material. Once you understand this, you can begin to use it to your advantage.

Therefore, if everything about us is connected to the universe through energy, it only makes sense that our desires, fears, deeply held beliefs, affirmations and repeated images have an effect on the reality of our present lives.

Visualizations

We live in a boundless quantum sea of pulsating energy that responds to what and how we think. Every thought that we have is a creative force and they are continuously expressing themselves in our lives. Once you come to a clear understanding of this concept, you can start to design your life in the way that you want, free from all negativity.

I'm sure you are asking by now how you can use this creative power? Good question, the answer is very simple. By using your mind to focus on what you desire, you can create the life that you want. The very first technique you will need to learn is visualization.

What is Visualization?

The basics of visualization is to rehearse what you want mentally. You can create the images in your mind of what you want to happen in your life. You will then need to spend five minutes every day seeing yourself performing that which you desire. The idea here is that you attract whatever you focus on, the key to effective visualization is to visualize that you have already achieved what you want. You don't focus on hoping to get it, or on desiring to get it, you focus on getting it. You have to live it and feel it within your mind as if you already have it and that you are living in it at that moment. Your conscious mind knows that you are playing a mental trick, but your subconscious mind is unable to distinguish between what is real and what is fake; therefore, your subconscious mind will take action based on the images that you create whether or not they reflect your present reality or not.

John Kehoe, a mind power expert has been teaching this skill for many years and has seen it come to pass in the lives of millions. It is important to remember that this isn't some type of magic trick, you are not going to see results overnight, but if you are persistent in your vision it will become a reality in your life. You can achieve whatever you want out of life once you understand the power of the mind.

Affirmations

People who are bound in a negative lifecycle are in their predicament because they have talked themselves into it through the inner dialogue that takes place within the mind. An affirmation is a statement that you either speak to yourself out loud or in your mind. If you are constantly telling yourself "You will never amount to anything," that is exactly what you are going to get out of life. If you are about to have a job interview and you tell yourself "I will never get the job," don't be surprised when you receive that rejection letter through the mail.

Why do Affirmations Work

Whatever you say to yourself has a direct influence on your thoughts. This is the main reason why affirmations are so powerful. If you tell yourself that you are going to have a good interview, you will automatically start to think about how great your interview is going to be. You attract whatever you focus on, so start using affirmations to focus on what you desire. When you are using affirmations, there are three rules you will need to remember:

1. **Stay Positive:** Reject every thought that doesn't line up with what you want, thoughts such as "What if I say the wrong thing in the interview?" or thinking

thoughts such as, "I'm afraid of what's going to happen today." Statements like these keep your mind focused on the things you don't want as opposed to what you do want. Everything that you affirm should be based on what you want.

2. **Short and Simple:** There is no need to have some long winded and convoluted affirmations, use one sentence or a short phrase. View your affirmation as a mantra that you say to yourself continuously without even thinking about it.

3. **Don't Try and Believe it:** You don't have to believe what you are saying, that will come later as it begins to have an effect on your subconscious mind. Continuously repeating the statement will cause it to come to pass in your life.

Affirmations are extremely powerful, simple and easy to use. Professional athletes worldwide use them to enhance their performance. Business people use them to run their businesses successfully and close deals, artists use them to think about innovative new ideas and to be creative and you can use them to overcome negative emotional issues.

Chapter 3: Anxiety and Cognitive Behavioral Therapy

Anxiety is an emotion experienced by everyone for various reasons. When we have an important decision to make, when sitting an exam, or when dealing with unsettling issues at home or at work. Under such circumstances it is only normal that you are going to feel anxious. However; the condition referred to as "Anxiety disorder" is a crippling illness that negatively affects millions of people worldwide. It can cause excessive stress levels which can affect an individual's everyday life. It is a severe mental disorder that causes continuous overwhelming fear and worry.

There are a variety of anxiety disorders, these include the following:

Panic Disorder: Feelings of sudden terror that manifest without warning and for no reason. These feelings are most commonly known as a "panic attack," physical symptoms include irregular or strong heartbeat, a feeling of being choked, sweating or chest pains. Sufferers compare the feeling to the inability to control the mind, and similar to a heart attack.

Social Anxiety Disorder: This type of anxiety is also known as "social phobia." Sufferers experience extreme fear about being in everyday social situations. It is often described as a constant paranoia that no one likes them.

Specific Phobias: When individuals experience extreme fear of situations or objects. This can include heights or flying. Some individuals are known to fear things such as door handles or windows. Such phobias will often lead people to avoid doing things such as visiting friends or going to work.

Generalized Anxiety Disorder: This is an unrealistic, exaggerated worry and tension about situations that have been imagined in the mind. None of the situations actually exist physically; they are all the result of the imagination.

Symptoms are dependent on the type of anxiety; however, the typical symptoms include the following:

- Sleeping problems
- Dizzyness
- Cold or sweaty hands and feet
- Restlessness
- Heart palpitations
- Shortage of breath
- Dry mouth
- Feelings of panic
- Muscle tension
- Nausea
- Numbness or tingling in the hands and feet

The medical community are still searching for the cause of anxiety disorders. However, like any type of mental illness, the condition is not a result of a character flaw, poor upbringing and weakness. As scientists continue to look into the causes of such conditions it is becoming apparent that there are a variety of factors that contribute to the condition such as a chemical imbalance in the brain, stress and environmental pressures.

How to Eliminate Anxiety With Cognitive Behavioral Therapy

The key to overcoming anxiety is having the ability to deal with the anxious thoughts. Here are some methods to assist you:

What is the source of your anxiety: Whether you have a full blown panic attack or a sudden bout of fear or worry, it is important to know where your anxiety is coming from. Is there something in your environment that is causing it? An activity that you are going to have to attend? When you are clear about what the fear is you can handle the anxiety a lot easier.

Can you solve the problem: Once you have worked out what your fear is, the next step is to work out whether or not it is something that you can resolve. If the fear is something that you have imagined, you are going to have to make a conscious decision to stop thinking about it. If you can handle the situation you will need to take the appropriate steps to do so. Consider the following:

- What can you do to reduce the worry or fear?
- Is the solution long or short term?
- How can you prevent the fear or worry from resurfacing?

Worst Case Scenario: Maybe you are getting ready to do a presentation, or go for a job interview and you are worried about the outcome. When you start panicking, stop and think about the worst thing that can happen in that situation. Once you have made up in your mind that the worst that can happen in the interview is that your mind goes blank or in the presentation that you fall off the stage, you will start to calm down because the worst really isn't that bad after all.

Accept That You Are Not in Control: It can be difficult to stop worrying when you are not sure of how a situation is going to play itself out. However, once you come to the realization that there are some things that you simply have no control over and that worrying about the unknown is pointless your anxiety will alleviate.

Is Your Worry Useful? Sometimes it is useful to worry if you are faced with a real threat. When you are worrying stop and think about why you are worried, is there a legitimate reason for it or are you simply conjuring up imaginations in your mind. If there is no purpose behind your worrying then you can determine that you are not in a good place.

Focus on the positive and the negative: When you are feeling anxious about something it is easy to look at the negative side of the picture. As with everything, there are always two sides to every story. Focus on the positive aspects of your situation as well.

Avoid all or nothing thinking: No matter what is about to happen, it is highly unlikely that the outcome is going to be totally black or white. Don't permit yourself to ignore the grey areas and don't over-exaggerate things. For example, just say you didn't get into the college that you wanted to go to; you immediately start to think that you are a complete failure and no college is going to accept you. This thinking is common with people who suffer from anxiety and it is completely irrational.

Don't turn things into a catastrophe: When anxiety brings on fear there is a tendency to turn the event into a major catastrophe in your mind. For example, if you are scared of flying and you experience turbulence on the plane, you immediately start thinking that the plane is going to blow up. This type of thinking will only intensify your anxiety.

Avoid jumping to conclusions: If you don't have enough facts and you have not yet experienced the fear or the worry that you are imagining don't jump to conclusions. This will not do you any good. If you are uncertain about something you can eliminate anxiety by admitting to yourself that you don't know what is going to happen. Instead of jumping to the most unlikely or the most morbid, think of all possible outcomes.

Don't allow your emotions to control your reasoning: When you are anxious or scared it's easy to allow your emotions to get in the way of your logic. Your emotions will only fool you into thinking that you are faced with more harm than you actually are. Don't allow the fear of the unknown to convince you that you are in harm's way.

Avoid making it personal: When people get anxious, they will often start to blame themselves for situations that are outside of their control. If you are scared and anxious because your house has been broken into, it can be easy to blame yourself and take it personally. This is an illogical thought process and it will make you feel even worse. Unless you opened the door to the thieves and gave them permission to help themselves you can't hold yourself accountable for anything that went missing.

Self exposure therapy: This technique is slightly complicated but it works. If you are brave enough you can try this on your own. The main aim of exposure therapy is that when the brain is exposed to something for a long period of time the individual will no longer be afraid of it. The best way to understand this technique is to think of it in terms of a phobia. For example, if you are scared of spiders you would do the following:

- Force yourself to think about spiders continuously, this is going to stress you out but don't try and fight against it. Allow yourself to be stressed and keep thinking about the spiders until you feel yourself relax. Keep doing this for several days in a row until you no longer get stressed when you think about spiders.

- Your next step will be to print out a photo of a spider, keep looking at the photo until you feel yourself relax. Keep doing this for several days in a row until you are no longer fearful when you look at the spiders.

- Your next step will be to watch videos on YouTube of spiders, keep watching them until you no longer feel anxious.

- Your next step will be to have a friend catch a spider and put it in a jar. You will then need to look at it for extended periods of time. Keep doing this until you no longer feel anxious about looking at the spider.

- Your next step will be to interact with the spider; you can do so by feeding it, or stroking it. When you are able to do this without feeling fearful you have overcome your phobia.

Although this is an example using a phobia you can also use the same technique for any type of anxiety. All types of anxiety have a trigger; panic attacks are typically triggered by a physical sensation. For example, if you get panic attacks as a result of feeling dizzy then spin around and feel dizzy on purpose. The idea is that the exposure to feeling dizzy will eliminate your fear of dizziness which leads to the panic attack.

Deep breathing exercises: When you are having an anxiety attack your breathing speeds up, this leads to a reduction in oxygen to the brain. When there isn't enough oxygen circulating in the brain it becomes difficult to think clearly and make logical decisions. When you start feeling anxious focus on your breathing. Inhale for four seconds and then exhale for four seconds, repeat this for two minutes and you should start to feel your nerves calm down.

Exercise: Physical activity stimulates the release of the feel good hormone endorphins which improves your mood. It also reduces the stress hormone cortisol. As soon as you start to feel yourself getting anxious go for a walk or work out.

Meditation or prayer: When you make a conscious decision to take your focus off the negative thoughts that are causing you to feel anxious and focus on gaining inner peace your fears and anxiety will quickly alleviate. When you start feeling anxious focus your energy inwards and pray or repeat a positive mantra. Focus on this entirely and eventually your anxiety will disappear.

A healthy diet: What you eat plays a major role in your mental capabilities. Studies have shown that there is a direct relationship between high levels of stress and anxiety and healthy eating. The first thing you should do is to get tested to ensure that you are not suffering from any food allergies that trigger anxiety. Your next step is to incorporate more fruit, vegetables and whole grains into your diet.

Magnesium supplements: Magnesium is known to alleviate anxiety. If you suffer from a magnesium deficiency you are going to be more worried and anxious than normal. You can get magnesium supplements from your local health food store.

Herbal remedies: There have been many scientific studies that have discovered that certain herbs such as chamomile, valerian root, and St. Johns wort can relieve anxiety symptoms.

Chapter 4: Addiction and Cognitive Behavioral Therapy

For over five years Dave watched his son Noel battle with methamphetamine addiction. By the age of 27, Noel had been to several different rehab and treatment programs, some of them helped in the short term but he would always end up relapsing and back on the streets and his parents were back to square one, terrified with nowhere to turn.

At this point Dave had given up on the healthcare system helping his son. As a journalist he started to write a book about addiction and began to interview some of the world's leading experts about the nature of addiction and treatment. Dave says that he was at his wits end, he was interviewing someone who knew more about the methamphetamine addiction than anyone else in the world but even he was unable to tell him where he could get the help that he needed. He asked other researchers and work colleges, but still no answer.

Since the experts didn't know, he decided to change his approach and began to interview people who had overcome addiction to find out how they did it. That was when he met Holly, addicted to methamphetamine for 15 years; she described herself as racked with demons she was unable to control. Holly went through the same ordeal, treatment center after treatment center yet nothing seemed to work. Until one day she was introduced to cognitive behavioral therapy, she was at the end of the line and believed she would die if she didn't quit. She has now been clean for 12 years.

Holly's success story inspired Dave to send Noel to one of the best cognitive behavioral therapists in the United States. Today Noel is 32 years old, five years clean, happily married and the author of two books about overcoming addiction. According to Dave his experience mirrors the medical field's lack of understanding concerning the problem of addiction and their ability to effectively treat it.

Today over 40 million Americans suffer from some type of addiction, whether its drug, alcohol or nicotine addiction. According to the National Center on Addiction and Substance abuse less than 10 percent receive treatment, and even less receive effective treatment. The last few decades have seen researchers develop effective behavioral and pharmaceutical treatments for addiction. However, in community and residential treatment programs such treatments are scarce and programs typically involve strategies such as "tough love" tactics which are rarely effective. There are also the most popular treatment programs that the majority of people have heard of Narcotics Anonymous and Alcoholics anonymous which have helped many addicts at the same time as failing many others.

There are many reasons for the treatment failures for addiction in America. These include a long history of viewing drug addiction as a moral failure as opposed to a disease. The health insurance industry has no interest in covering addiction, and a state wide problem of licensing standards that often do not require addiction counselors to have a great deal of training to effectively handle the problems that addicts deal with.

What Works

There are several forms of evidence-based behavioral treatments for substance abuse and cognitive behavioral therapy is one of the most strongly supported. Before you start working on the following techniques you will need to prepare yourself for change. Here are the five key steps that you will need to follow:

1. Write down the reasons why you want to change
2. If you have attempted recovery previously why didn't it work?
3. Set yourself measurable goals such as a start date to begin.

4. Remove all reminders of your addiction from your workplace, home or anywhere else you visit frequently
5. Let your friends and family know that you are committed to recovery and ask them for your support

Get a Support Network

Don't attempt to fight your addiction alone, it is essential that you have a solid support system and positive influences. The more people you have to turn to for guidance, a listening ear and encouragement the better.

Family and Friends: The support of family and friends is invaluable when it comes to recovery. If you don't feel comfortable turning to family because you have let them down in the past you might want to consider family therapy or relationship counseling to patch things up.

Build a Network of Sober Friends: Like typically attracts like so there is a high possibility that you have a lot of friends that are not sober.

It is essential that you break free from this group of people because they will set you up for failure. It's important that you have sober friends that will walk you through your recovery. You might want to join a church, take a class, volunteer, or attend events in your community so that you can build your network.

Sober Living Home: You might want to consider moving into a sober living home if you don't have a drug free living environment or a stable home.

Go to Meetings: A recovery support group will provide you with the encouragement that you need to persevere with your recovery. It can be extremely therapeutic to spend time in the presence of people who understand what you are going through.

What Led to Your Addiction: Addiction doesn't just happen, there is always an underlying cause and it is essential that you find out what it is to ensure that it doesn't resurface. Did you start using to eliminate memories from a traumatic event? A breakdown of a relationship? If you don't deal with the root of the problem it will only resurface once you are sober. In order for the treatment to be successful you will first need to deal with the underlying causes.

When you have resolved the underlying issues, you are going to experience bouts of anxiety, shame, anger, frustration, loneliness and stress. These emotions are normal but you will need to find ways to handle them as a part of your treatment.

Stress Relief: Many people turn to drugs or alcohol as a way of relieving stress, or to forget about painful events that have happened in life. There are much better ways that you can alleviate stress. You can learn to effectively manage your problems without reverting back to your addiction. Everyone is different; therefore, you will need to find the best techniques that work well for you. When you are confident about dealing with stress you will find that it is not as overwhelming and intimidating to handle it.

Exercise: Meditation and yoga are great ways to alleviate stress; you can also take a quick walk around the block.

Get some sun: Just being exposed to nature will quickly calm you down.

Play with an animal: Animals can soothe and relax you.

Smell: Breath in the scent of a flower, your favorite perfume or some fresh coffee beans.

Visualize: Take yourself out of the moment and visualize being in a beautiful scene.

Pamper yourself: Soak in a hot bath, or take a long shower, you can also give yourself a shoulder or a neck massage.

Triggers and Cravings: Getting sober is not the end of your recovery; your brain still needs time to rebuild the connections that were distorted while you were an addict. During the rebuilding process you will have some very intense drug cravings. You are going to have to make sure that you stay away from situations, people and places that trigger the temptation to use.

Coping Strategies: Cravings are going to come and they can't be avoided; therefore, it is essential that you already have coping strategies prepared:

Distracting activities: There are many things that you can do to distract yourself, these include: exercise, hike, a hobby, read, watch a movie or go and see a friend. Once your focus is on something else, you will find that the urges go away.

Talk it out: When your cravings occur, talk to sober friends or family members. Talking can help you to pinpoint the source of the craving and it can also help you to relieve the feeling.

Urge Surf: A lot of addicts try and cope with their cravings by just experiencing them. Some cravings are so strong that they are impossible to ignore. When this happens, it can be helpful to hold on to the urge until it passes. This technique is referred to as urge surfing, imagine that you are a surfer who is riding the wave of your craving, keeping on top of it until it breaks, crests, and loses its power.

Change and Challenge Your Thoughts: When addicts are experiencing a craving they have a tendency to remember how good the drug made them feel and forget about the negative consequences. You might find it helpful to remind yourself how bad the drug made you feel once you had come down off the high.

Chapter 5: Depression and Cognitive Behavioral Therapy

What is Depression?

According to the American Psychiatric Association depression is serious but common medical condition. It affects the way you act, think and feel; fortunately, the condition is treatable. Depression causes individuals to become extremely sad and to lose interest in activities they once found enjoyable. It can lead to a range of physical and emotional problems that affect a person's ability to function at home and at work.

The symptoms of depression range from mild to extreme and can include:

- A low mood and the feeling of sadness
- A loss of pleasure and interest in activities once enjoyed
- A change in appetite leading to either weight loss or weight gain

- The inability to sleep or excessive sleeping
- Increased tiredness and lack of energy
- An increase in meaningless activity such as pacing and wringing of hands
- Slowed speech and movements
- Feeling guilty or worthless
- Difficulty concentrating, thinking or making decisions
- Thoughts of suicide or death

For a diagnosis of depression, symptoms must last for more than two weeks. Also, medical conditions such as vitamin deficiency, brain tumor and thyroid problems must be ruled out. These conditions can imitate symptoms of depression.

Depression affects approximately 6.7% of American adults per year; an estimated 16.6% of people will experience depression at some time during their life. The condition can strike at any time, but it typically appears during the late teenage years or the mid-20s. Depression is more common in women than it is in men. Several studies have found that one-third of all women will experience a major episode of depression at some time within their life.

What Depression is Not

The end of a relationship, the loss of a job, and the death of a loved one are all traumatic experiences for an individual to experience. In such situations, it is normal for a person to feel grief or sadness and people will often describe themselves as feeling "depressed" when they go through such events. However, feeling sad is not the same as suffering from depression. The grieving process is natural and each individual will have their own unique experience which will mirror some of the characteristics of depression. Both depression and grief will involve feelings of deep sadness and a lack of interest in normal activities. However, they are also significantly different in the following ways:

- During grief, feelings of pain manifest in waves often intermingled with happy memories. You will often witness people laugh at the same time as crying as they remember some of the things that their loved one used to do. When a person is depressed, they experience a low mood for up to two weeks at a time.

- During grief, self esteem is typically maintained. When a person is depressed they generally feel worthless.

- For some people, major depression can be brought on by the death of a loved one. A major disaster, being a victim of a physical assault or losing a job can induce a major depression. When depression and grief exist together, the grief lasts longer and is more severe than when it isn't accompanied by depression. Although there is a slight overlap between depression and grief they are very different.

Depression Risk Factors

Depression doesn't discriminate; anyone can be affected by it regardless of the circumstances in which they live. The majority of people are unable to understand why the rich and famous get depressed when they appear to have everything in life. There is more to depression than lifestyle and circumstances.

- **Biochemistry:** A chemical imbalance in the brain can cause depression.

- **Genetics:** Depression can be hereditary, for example, if your mother suffered depression there is a 70 percent chance that you might experience it too.

- **Personality:** People who suffer from low self esteem, typically pessimistic, or easily overwhelmed by stress are more likely to suffer from depression.

- **Environmental Factors:** Continuous exposure to poverty, abuse, violence or neglect are more likely to suffer from depression.

How Depression is Treated With Cognitive Behavioral Therapy

Stay Connected: People who suffer from depression have a tendency to isolate themselves. It can be difficult to reach out to friends and family if you've been isolating yourself but a part of cognitive behavioral therapy is challenging yourself and doing the very things that make you feel uncomfortable. Social support is essential if you plan on recovering from depression. If you feel as if you don't have anyone to turn to, you can find a support network and make new friends. Here are some tips for staying connected:

- Talk to someone about how you feel
- Take the focus off yourself and help someone out by volunteering
- Have coffee or lunch with a friend
- Ask someone that you trust to check on you regularly

- Go to a concert, the movies, or a small get together with a friend
- Email or call an old friend
- Schedule weekly dinner with a friend or family member
- Join a club or a class so that you can meet new people
- Confide in a teacher or a clergy member

Participate in Activities That You Like

If you want to overcome depression you are going to have to start doing things that energize and relax you. This includes following a healthy diet and an exercise regime, learning how to effectively manage stress, set limits on what you can and can't do, and schedule activities that you enjoy each day.

While it's not possible to force yourself to experience pleasure or to have fun, you can force yourself to do things regardless of whether you feel like doing it or not. You will be surprised at how much better you feel once you actually get out there and start doing things. Even if the depression doesn't leave straight away, you will gradually start to feel more energetic and upbeat as you participate in activities that you enjoy. Here are some of things that you might want to consider:

- Get back into a sport or hobby that you used to enjoy
- Take a trip to the ballpark, mountains or museum
- Go out with friends
- Express yourself through art, music or writing

Get Enough Sleep: People who are depressed either find it too difficult to sleep or they don't get enough sleep. When your sleep is disturbed your mood suffers. Get yourself into a sleep wake cycle where you go to sleep and wake up at the same time every day.

Get Some Sun: When you are not exposed to the sun it can make depression worse. Get at least 15 minutes of sunlight each day to boost your mood. You can go for a short walk, have your meal or a coffee outside, or sit on a park bench and people watch.

Relaxation Techniques: Practicing relaxation techniques can reduce stress, boost feelings of well being and joy, and alleviate symptoms of depression. Try meditation, progressive muscle relaxation, deep breathing or yoga.

Create a Wellness Toolbox

Write out a list of things that you can do to quickly boost your mood. The more tools that you have for coping with depression the better. Try and implement a couple of these ideas every day even if you are feeling okay.

- Spend more time outdoors
- List the things that you like about yourself
- Read a book that you know is good
- Watch a funny TV show or movie
- Take a hot bath
- Play with an animal

- Talk to family and friends face to face
- Listen to music
- Do something that's out of the ordinary to you

Exercise: When you're depressed it can be a difficult task just to get out of bed let alone work out. However, exercise is a powerful way to fight depression. Research has discovered that regular exercise can be as effective as medication for alleviating symptoms of depression. It can also help to prevent you from relapsing once you have fully recovered.

In order to get the most benefit from exercise you will need to get a minimum of 30 minutes exercise each day. You should aim to do exercise that is rhythmic and continuous; this includes dancing, martial arts, swimming, weight training and walking.

Healthy Eating: The foods that you eat have a direct impact on the way you feel. You should eliminate foods that have an adverse effect on your mood and brain such as trans fats, caffeine, alcohol and foods that are high in chemical preservatives.

Don't Skip Meals: You shouldn't wait too long between meals because this will make you feel tired and irritable. You should aim to eat every four hours.

Limit Carbs and Refined Sugars: Feel good foods such as French fries, pasta, baked goods or sugary snacks lead to a quick crash in energy and mood.

Your depression isn't going to go away overnight; however, if you follow the advice provided in this chapter consistently you will start to notice a dramatic improvement in your bouts of depression.

Chapter 6: Negative Thinking and Cognitive Behavioral Therapy

Do you always focus on the criticisms and forget about the compliments? Do you spend significant amounts of time going over previous mistakes? If you have answered yes to any of these questions, it is more than likely that you are trapped in a cycle of negative thinking.

For some people happiness is a very short lived experience until those negative thoughts and feelings begin to beat you back into your comfortable reality. If you are continuously bombarded with negative thoughts, don't just assume you have a bad habit. Negative events tend to plague people longer than positive events. It is human nature to spend more time trying to work out why something went wrong so that the same mistakes are not made again in future. In such instances an individual is simply being realistic as opposed to exhibiting patterns of negative thinking.

However, if your negative thinking is having an adverse affect on your life you will need to take the required steps to handle them.

The Cycle of Negative Thinking

According to scientists, there is a neurological explanation for the cycle of negative thinking. The amygdala is the part of the brain that is responsible for our emotional state. When it is aroused it remains in that state for an extended period of time. The brain then captures a memory of the situation and the stronger the emotion, the more powerful the memory.

As time goes on, emotions and memories become attached to one another. For example, the feeling of nervousness may trigger the memory of being sacked from a job years ago. This feeling remains as you continue to remember the negative experience. When this continues for an extended period of time it is referred to as "flooding," this is where you begin to dwell on several negative circumstances one after the other.

How Does Negative Thinking Develop

The way we were raised plays a key part in our thinking patterns. Every mother and father has their own unique parenting style. Some may feel it necessary to explain the potential dangers in every situation in an attempt safeguard their children. This can lead to anxiety as their child grows up expecting the worst to happen in every situation which then develops into a negative view of the world.

Parents who are excessively critical towards their children can lead them to adopt a negative state of mind. It may be that you were raised in a household with a long list of "musts" and "shoulds," which means that you now find it difficult to relax. Here is a list of the most common negative thinking traps:

- **Musts and Shoulds:** When you tell yourself not to do something it actually increases the likelihood of you doing it. That voice of command belonged to your parents, as an adult you are now in charge of your life.

- **All or nothing:** Just because you failed in something once doesn't mean that you are always going to fail or that life has a hit out against you. Avoid making over generalizations by using words such as "never" and "always."

- **Negative labeling:** "I won't succeed at anything, if people knew who I really was they would hate me."

- **The Inability to Recognize the Positive Aspects of Your Life:** "Nothing good ever happens to me, my life is awful."

- **Exaggerated thinking:** Always thinking that the worst has happened. For example, your friend is 10 minutes late to meet you because she got stuck in traffic but you think she's late because deep down she doesn't really like you.

- **Personalization:** Anything negative that happens, whether in your life or someone else's is always because of something that you have done.

How to Overcome Negative Thinking Using CBT

Nobody takes pleasure in negative thinking, it can make you feel depressed and anxious and prevent you from living the life that you deserve. Here are some techniques that you can use to eliminate negative thinking.

Thought Stopping

In order to stop thoughts that are not benefiting you, identify the thought, focus on it and then to end the thought say "Stop." When you first start this technique you will shout "Stop" out loud. You will then learn to say it in silence so that you can use the technique no matter where you are. Here is how you can begin:

1. **List the thoughts that bother you the most:** These are the thoughts that

keep you from working on your daily tasks and make you worry continuously. You want these thoughts to stop but they keep coming back to you. Write these thoughts down in order, from the most stressful to the least. Begin to practice thought stopping with the thought that bothers you the least.

2. **Thought imagination:** Find a private place where no one is going to disturb you and no one will be able to hear you and sit or lie down. Shut your eyes and think about a situation where you might have this distressing thought. You will then need to allow yourself to keep your focus on that thought.

3. **Stop the thought:** Shocking yourself is a good way to interrupt the thought. You can try with one of these two techniques:

- Set an alarm for 3 minutes and then focus on the thoughts that you don't want. When the alarm sounds, shout "Stop!" You can also stand up when you say "Stop." Some people clap their hands or snap their fingers. The combination of the actions and saying "Stop" are the cues you need to stop thinking. At this point you will need to empty your mind without thinking about anything for 30 seconds. During this time, if the unwanted thought returns shout "Stop!" again.

- Instead of using an alarm, you can record yourself shouting "Stop!" at 3, 2 and 1 minute intervals. Begin the exercise by focusing on the distressing thought and when you hear your voice shout "Stop!" snap out of thinking about the distressing thought. When you hear your own voice prompting you to stop it will strengthen your commitment to get rid of the unwanted thought.

Practice each of the steps until the thought goes away automatically, you will then need to start the process again. This time when you say the "Stop!" don't shout, say it in a normal tone.

Once a normal tone is able to stop the thought, you will then need to move onto whispering the word "Stop." After some time of practicing the activity, begin to say "Stop!" silently in your mind.

Continue with this process and move up the list until you get to your worst thought.

Different Thought Stopping Techniques

- Place a rubber band around your wrist and whenever you want to get rid of an unwanted thought say "Stop" quietly to yourself at the same time as snapping the rubber band. After you have practiced this for a while you will be able to snap the rubber band any time you get a negative thought without having to say "stop."

- Bring yourself into awareness of the fact that you are having a negative thought by speaking to yourself out loud to alert you to the fact that this is something that you are thinking about and it's not actually happening. You can say something like, "I'm having a negative thought that I'm going to lose my job."

- Once you have got rid of the negative thought you can replace it with a positive thought or image that will make you feel calm or relaxed.

Self Statements: You already know what your major negative thoughts are, another technique involves writing out a self statement to cancel out each negative thought that you have. Carry these self statements around with you wherever you go. Whenever you hear that voice in your head trying to suffocate you with negative thoughts repeat your self statements. After some time your mind will become used to replacing the negative thoughts with the positive ones.

The self-statement shouldn't be too far removed from the negative thought or the mind will find it too difficult to accept. For example, if your negative thought is "I'm so fat and ugly," instead of having a self statement like, "I'm the most beautiful girl in the world," you can say "I know I'm not perfect but I've got a lot of good qualities that I'm proud of." The message tells you that it's okay to feel happy, at the same time your mind isn't forced to prepare itself for disappointment when it realizes that what you are saying isn't true.

After some time, your self-statements can become redundant and you will need to change them.

Find Opportunities to Think Positive: People with a negative thought pattern will often walk into a room and immediately search for things that they don't like. For example, they will moan about the curtains, or the color of the carpet. If you know that this sounds like something you do train yourself to find five things in the room that you like instead. You can also set your phone three times per day to remind you that you need to think positive. If you have a friend who is also trying to change the way they think you can partner up with them and encourage each other.

End Each Day on a Positive Note: Instead of going to bed thinking about all of the bad things that have taken place during the day go to bed and reflect on the good that has taken place. This will reprogram your mind to focus on the positive aspects of your life instead of the negative.

Conclusion

Congratulations! You made it to the end of the book. I hope that you have been encouraged to overcome every challenge that you have endured. As you have read, cognitive behavioral therapy isn't a quick fix; you are going to have to work on your mind for the rest of your life to ensure that you don't regress. The more you put these exercises into practice the easier it will become for you to overcome the difficulties that you face in life.

Perseverance, determination and dedication are essential if you want to be completely free, how hard you choose to work is up to you.

I wish you all the best on your journey to emotional freedom!

Other books available by D.C. Johnson on Kindle, paperback and audio:

Are You In A Toxic Relationship? How to Let Go and Move On With Your Life